Families Through Time

Jeanne Dustman, M.A.Ed.

Consultants

Shelley Scudder
Gifted Education Teacher
Broward County Schools

Caryn Williams, M.S.Ed.
Madison County Schools
Huntsville, AL

Publishing Credits

Conni Medina, M.A.Ed., *Managing Editor*
Lee Aucoin, *Creative Director*
Torrey Maloof, *Editor*
Marissa Rodriguez, *Designer*
Stephanie Reid, *Photo Editor*
Rachelle Cracchiolo, M.S.Ed., *Publisher*

Image Credits: Cover, pp. 1, 2–3, 29(bottom) Thinkstock; pp. 5, 7, 9, 20, 21, 23, 25, 26, 28, 29 (top) Alamy; pp. 15, 19 Associated Press; p. 17 Corbis; pp. 14, 22, 24, 32 Getty Images; p. 6 Jeanne Dustman; pp. 8, 12, 16, 18 The Granger Collection; p. 4 The Library of Congress [LC-USZ6-1827]; p. 10 The Library of Congress [LC-DIG-fsa-8b30017]; All other images from Shutterstock.

Teacher Created Materials
5301 Oceanus Drive
Huntington Beach, CA 92649-1030
http://www.tcmpub.com

ISBN 978-1-4333-6991-9

Printed by: 584728 Printed In: India PO#:16147

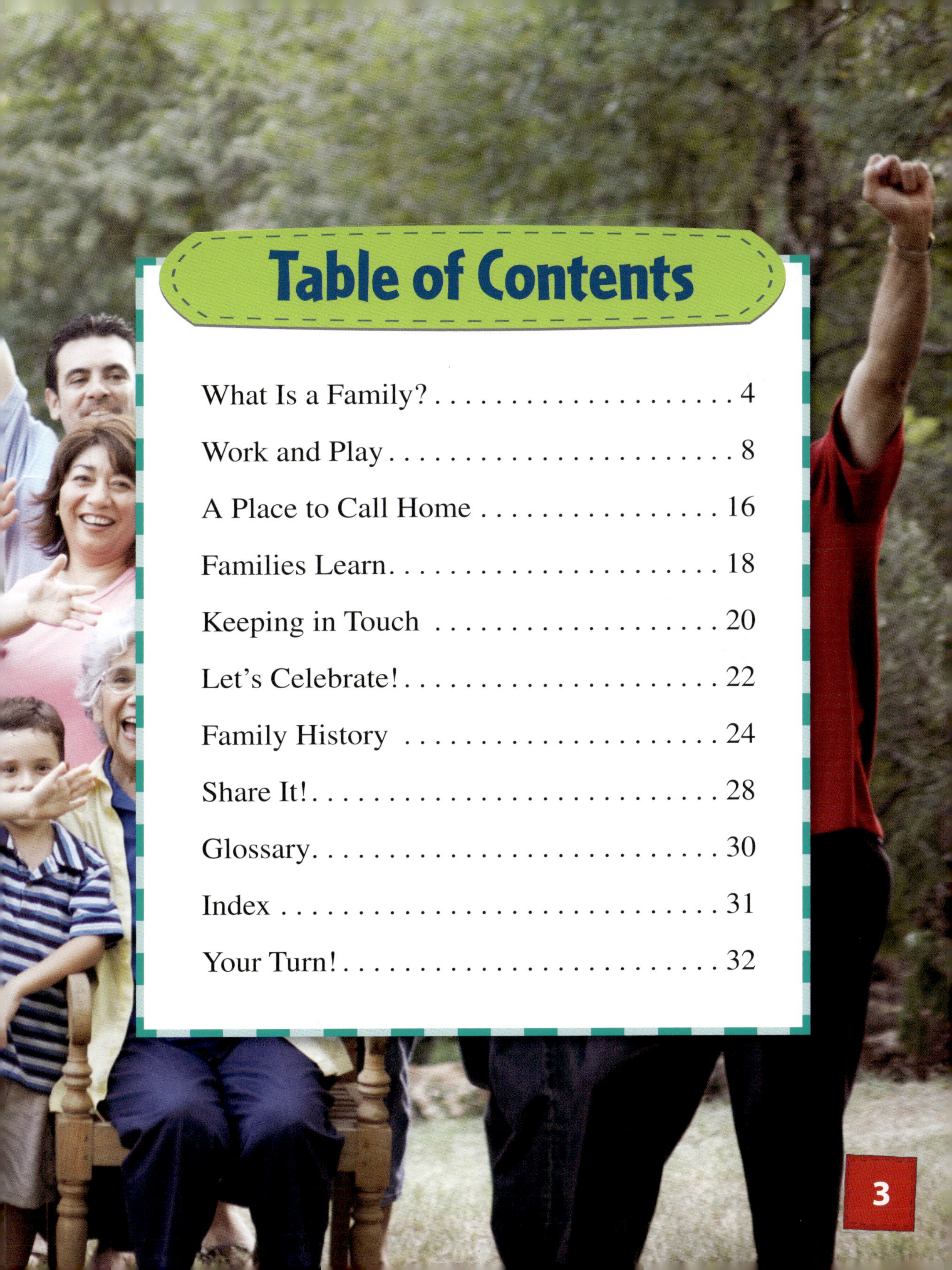

Table of Contents

This is a big family from long ago.

What Is a Family?

What is a family? A family is a group of people who love one another. They help one another. They keep one another safe.

This is a small family today.

There are many types of families. Some are big. Others are small. Some have people who are **related** to one another. They are connected through birth, adoption, or marriage. Others have people who are not related to one another. They may be connected in other ways.

Some families have mothers and fathers. Some have sisters and brothers. Some have grandparents. Some have aunts and uncles. Some also have cousins. Some families even have pets!

This family has two pets.

But a family does not need to have all of these people. It can be two people who take care of each other. Or it can be 10 people who take care of one another. The number of people is not important.

This family has a mother, two daughters, and a pet horse.

Work and Play

In the past, families worked long hours each day. There was a lot to do at home. Everyone had to help. There were no **machines** (muh-SHEENZ) such as vacuums (VAK-yoomz) to help keep the house clean. Kids had to help, too.

This family works on its farm long ago.

Today, machines make it easier to keep the house clean. Kids still help around the house, but they also have time to go to school and have fun.

This boy helps clean the house.

Families used to grow and make all of their own food. They spent a lot of time in their gardens and kitchens. Bread was baked in the oven. Butter was churned, or stirred, by hand.

This girl is churning butter in 1939.

Today, families can buy food at a grocery store. They can also buy meals at restaurants. Families have more time today because they do not have to make all of their food. They can use this time for work or fun.

This family is eating at a restaurant.

Long ago, families had to make their own clothes. Women often made the clothes for their families. This took a long time and was hard work.

This woman is making clothes in 1907.

Then, **factories** came along. Factories are places where things are made. They made clothes quickly and easily. People opened clothing stores. Trains brought clothes from factories to stores everywhere. Today, most families buy their clothes in stores.

Online Shopping

Most stores have websites where people can buy things while at home. Today, people can buy their clothes online.

This family is shopping online.

This family is having fun on a boat in 1950.

In the past, families had to work most of the time. But they had fun together, too. Families played games. They sang songs. They also visited their **relatives** and friends. They enjoyed the outdoors. Kids played with their friends and pets, too.

This family is camping.

Today, families still find ways to spend time together. They play video games. They take trips. They travel in airplanes and in cars.

A Place to Call Home

A home is a place a family lives. It is where a family eats and sleeps. A home is where a family has **celebrations** (sel-uh-BREY-shuhnz). Celebrations are parties for special days. A family makes **memories** in a home. Memories are things people remember about the past.

This family built a house long ago.

Long ago, families had to build their own homes. Today, most families do not build their homes. They buy or rent them from other people. Some homes are for one family. Others live in buildings with many families. But the best thing about a home is that a family lives in it.

This family bought a house.

Long ago, many kids learned at home.

Families Learn

Long ago, many kids did not have time to go to school. Kids who lived in the country needed to help with farming and chores. They would learn at home. Kids who lived in the city often went to school to learn. These kids did not have as many chores at home. They had more time to learn.

Today children go to school.

Today, the **law** says that all kids have to go to school. Some kids can go to school at home. This is called *homeschooling*. Kids who are homeschooled have to show that they are learning as much as kids who go to school.

Keeping in Touch

Years ago, members of a family often lived in the same town. They saw one another every day. Today, some relatives live far apart. They miss one another. But they find new ways to talk and keep in touch. People can call each other on phones. They can send emails, too.

Let's Talk!

Long ago, homes did not have telephones. People wrote letters to each other. Today, most people have cell phones and computers.

This family is talking on a phone.

Families also get together for **reunions**. They talk and share stories. This helps them stay close.

This is a family reunion.

Let's Celebrate!

Many families like to have celebrations. They may have celebrations for birthdays, holidays, or weddings. Celebrations may be large. They may be small. Celebrations are times for families to be happy.

This family is celebrating a birthday in 1953.

Many families like to celebrate with food. Some like to celebrate with games. Others like to celebrate with music and dancing. Celebrations help people stay in touch with their families. They help families make memories.

Party Time!

Americans celebrate many holidays. These include the Fourth of July, Mother's Day, and Thanksgiving.

This family likes to celebrate with food.

Family History

Families have **traditions** (truh-DISH-uhnz). Traditions are ways of doing things that have been done by a family for a long time. Families may have special recipes for holiday meals. Or, they may have a special song they sing each night.

This family is taking a drive in a car in 1960.

Each family has its own traditions. Sharing them is part of being a family. Kids learn about traditions from older family members. Traditions help us stay close to our past.

This grandfather is teaching his granddaughter how to write in Chinese.

Families share a history. Kids grow up. They have kids of their own. Mothers and fathers grow older. They become grandparents. Many things are the same for families today as long ago. Some things are not. We all change and grow.

This family likes spending time together.

Families come from many places. They look different. They have different traditions. But what makes all families the same is that they love one another.

My Family Story

The study of family history is called **genealogy** (jee-nee-OL-uh-jee). Your genealogy tells the story of your family through time.

This family tree shows the members of a family.

Share It!

Share your family's traditions with your friends. Ask about their families' traditions. How are the traditions different? How are they the same?

Glossary

celebrations—special or fun things people do for an important event or holiday

factories—places where things are made to be sold

genealogy—the history of a family

law—a rule made by the government

machines—things that people create to make jobs easier

memories—things people remember about the past

related—connected through birth, adoption, or marriage

relatives—members of a family

reunions—gatherings of people who have not been together for a long time

traditions—ways of thinking or doing things that have been used by a group of people or a family for a long time

Index

Your Turn!

Family Fun

This family is having fun on a boat. Families have fun together in different ways. How does your family have fun together? Draw a picture that shows your family having fun.